David Harmer was born in 1952. He has been the head teacher of Rosedale Primary School in Doncaster since ~~~8. His poems and stories for adults have appeared in ~~ magazines over the years. Most of his published ~~~ for children. He also writes stories for children. ~~~ been performing his poems since 1981. Currently ~~~ to be seen in the duo 'Spill the Beans' with Paul ~~~son at venues all over the country. He has also run ~~~ adult writing groups and has just completed an MA ~~~ing Studies at Sheffield Hallam University. David ~~~ Doncaster with his two children, Lizzie and ~~~nd his wife Paula. They have five cats, loads of ~~~ish and some frogs in the garden pond.

~~~es lives happily in London with her three boys – ~~~ Theo and Wilfred (husband, son and little black

Also available from Macmillan Children's Books

The Very Best of Paul Cookson

The Very Best of Wes Magee

The Very Best of Richard Edwards

The Very Best of Vernon Scannell

The Very Best of Ian McMillan

Elephant Dreams
Poems by Ian McMillan, David Harmer
and Paul Cookson

When the Teacher Isn't Looking
Poems chosen by David Harmer

Spill the Beans
Poems by David Harmer and Paul Cookson

THE VERY BEST OF...

DAVID HARMER

A Book of Poems

Illustrated by Jane Eccles

MACMILLAN CHILDREN'S BOOKS

For Paula, Lizzie and Harriet

First published 2001
by Macmillan Children's Books
a division of Pan Macmillan Ltd
20 New Wharf Road, London N1 9RR
Basingstoke and Oxford
www.panmacmillan.com

Associated companies throughout the world

ISBN 0 330 48190 8

Text copyright © David Harmer 2001
Illustrations copyright © Jane Eccles 2001

The right of David Harmer to be identified as the
author of this book has been asserted by him in accordance
with the Copyright, Designs and Patents Act 1988.

1 3 5 7 9 8 6 4 2

A CIP catalogue record for this book is available from the British Library.

Printed by Mackays of Chatham plc, Chatham, Kent.

Contents

Introduction   1
The Prime Minister Is Ten Today   5
Sir Guy Is in His Keep Tonight   7
On a Blue Day   8
The Space Explorer's Story   9
Mister Moore   10
Winter Morning: Winter Night   12
Some Days   14
Magic the Rabbit   15
Miss Smith's Garden Secret   16
Dobbo's First Swimming Lesson   17
Good Morning!   18
Diwali   19
Rudolph's Story   21
We Lost Our Teacher to the Sea   23
Barry's Budgie . . . Beware!   24
A Televised Surprise   25
My Dad's a Stuntman   26
What Marcus the Guard Did One Snowy Night   27
When Mum Takes Me Football Training   29
When Dad Took Me Football Training   31
Great-Gran Is Manic on Her Motorbike   33
The Inspectors' Report   34
The Lone Teacher   36
Lost in Space   38
Two Traffic Wardens Talking on Christmas Eve   39
Alone   41
My Mum's Put Me on the Transfer List   43
Our Tree   44
Will It Go to a Replay?   45
Funny Faces   47
Who Is My Neighbour?   49
Sir Guy and the Enchanted Princess   51

What the Mountains Do 53
Lion 54
All of Us Knocking on the Stable Door 55
Nights Out with Gaz 57
There's Very Little Merit in a Ferret 59
Dazzling Derek 61
Living with Cats 63
I'm a Shepherd in the Christmas Play 66
Busy Brothers, Talented Twins 68
I Want to Be Friends with a Girl Who . . . 70
I Want to Be Friends with a Boy Who . . . 72
The Elephant Dictionary 74
Alien Exchange 76
It's Behind You 78
There's a Monster in the Garden 80
Pasting Patsy's Pasty Posters 82
Flight from Planet Earth 83
The Visitor 84
Harry Hobgoblin's Superstore 86
Slick Nick's Dog's Tricks 88
Index of First Lines 89

Introduction

I always wanted to be a writer. Mind you, I always wanted to be one of the Beatles, play cricket for England, star in my own Hollywood movie and be Bob Dylan's best mate. Those things didn't work out so well, but I did get to be a writer. I started when I was at school, reading everything I could find and writing poems and stories (lots of those) and plays. Like Dylan Thomas once said, 'It's what school exercise books are for.' I knew about him because my mum is Welsh and she'd read me his work and my dad would buy me books, and between them they fed the flames. I was on fire for words.

At school I showed my first poems to a brilliant English teacher called John Fordham. He didn't fall about laughing, in fact he encouraged me to write some more. So I did. Later, when I was at college, I showed some more poems to a friend called John Williams. He said I should keep on going. Then, my pal Ian McMillan said the same. I decided to believe them and I carried on writing.

As I grew up writing and reading I made two wonderful discoveries. The first one is that poems don't have to rhyme. I know that it's blindingly obvious but you'd be amazed how many grown-ups think otherwise. Of course, grown-ups think all sorts of ridiculous things. I should know, I am one most of the time.

I began to read poems by all sorts of poets: Seamus Heaney, William Shakespeare, William Carlos Williams, T. S. Eliot, Ian McMillan, Carol Ann Duffy, Roger McGough, Sylvia Plath, Ted Hughes, Emily Dickinson and a million others, and none of these poets used rhymes.

So I began to write poems that didn't rhyme.

Then I made the second wonderful discovery, which

was that poems, if they wanted to, could rhyme like mad! So, I read all the same poets I had read before and found that most of them made rhyming poems as well. I met Kit Wright and read his marvellous rhymes, which taught me a lot.

So I began to write poems that rhymed.

In the end, of course, I found out that poems come in all shapes, sizes and varieties. They are long or short, fat or thin, old or new, they rhyme or they don't. They tell stories, convey moods, sound like dreams or like songs. They can make you laugh, make you angry, make you cry, or all three. Despite all this wonderful variety, they all have the same thing happening; they are filled with fiery, fabulous, fizzing-like-cola words and ideas. They are just so exciting.

I write poems and stories for grown-ups and when I do that I feel very sensible and serious. Or I try to make them laugh. They end up in magazines and in books and I feel great. At other times, I write poems and stories for children, and I turn into a ten-year-old boy who wants other children to enjoy his poems and to read them for themselves. They end up in books too, like this one!

Many years ago, I got together with Ian McMillan, John Turner and Martyn Wiley and we started a poetry act called 'Circus of Poets'. We jumped about a lot and made people laugh and I found out how to write performance poems. That's when I wrote my poem about Mr Moore, the most frightening head teacher in the world. At that time of my life I was hiding in a secret camp deep in the South Yorkshire forests learning how to be a head teacher myself. It worked and I've been at Rosedale Primary School since 1988, which is great because I love it there.

After a few years the 'Circus' ran out of poetry juice but

luckily I met Paul Cookson. We started being 'Spill the Beans', doing our poetry show all over the country, as well as on television. Paul is an excellent poet and we really enjoy working together. It was at about this time that Macmillan Children's Books started using our poems in their publications. Also, I went to Sheffield Hallam University to learn more about writing. I earned an MA and lots of advice from my friend Archie Markham, the best teacher of writing I have ever met.

I've been lucky. I've met so many people over the years who have encouraged me to be a writer and to learn from them. But the most important people in my story I have saved until the end. They are my children Lizzie and Harriet, and my wife Paula. They listen to my poems and say which bits they like and which bits they don't. As well as that, they do other stuff around the place so that I have time to write. They just keep me going all the time.

Sometimes people ask me for advice about writing and all I can say is that anyone out there who wants to be a writer must read a lot of books, look hard at the work of other writers, learn from them and then write what you want to write. Find some friends who write poems too and show your ideas and writing with each other. That way you can be a writer too. You can start right now, today, this minute!

Hope you enjoy the book.

David Harmer

The Prime Minister Is Ten Today

This morning I abolished
homework, detention and dinner ladies.
I outlawed lumpy custard, school mashed spuds
and handwriting lessons.
From now on playtimes must last two hours
unless it rains, in which case we all go home
except the teachers who must do extra PE
outside in the downpour.

Whispering behind your hand in class
must happen each morning between ten and twelve,
and each child need only do
ten minutes' work in one school hour.

I've passed a No Grumpy Teacher law
so one bad word or dismal frown
from Mr Spite or Miss Hatchetface
will get them each a month's stretch
sharpening pencils and marking books
inside the gaol of their choice.

All headteachers are forbidden
from wearing soft-soled shoes,
instead they must wear wooden clogs
so you can hear them coming.
They are also banned from shouting
or spoiling our assembly by pointing
at the ones who never listen.

Finally, the schools must shut
for at least half the year
and if the weather's really sunny
the teachers have to take us all
to the seaside for the day.

If you've got some good ideas
for other laws about the grown-ups
drop me a line in Downing Street,
I'll always be glad to listen.
Come on, help me change a thing or two
before we all grow up
and get boring.

Sir Guy Is in His Keep Tonight

The twelfth of December 1231
terrible snows, darkness, no sun
the castle is cold, silent and grey
I'm here on my own
my wife and children far away
on a winter holiday.
I've spent all the morning jousting
knocking knights off their horses
then archery in the butts, some swordplay
but I'm on my own tonight, of course
I've got all my servants and soldiers
the fires burning bright
but I'm alone in the keep
on my own
tonight.

I can see them clearly
swarming over the curtain wall
flooding the inner bailey
the thousand ghosts of the thousand Saxons
my father and his father
slaughtered daily
the Saxons fought well, died hard
look at them cover the castle's yard
ghosts, grey in the moonlight
bearded warriors of yesterday
coming for me
tonight.

On a Blue Day

On a blue day
when the brown heat
scorches the grass
and stings my legs with sweat

I go running like a fool
up the hill towards the trees
and my heart beats loudly
like a kettle boiling dry.

I need a bucket the size of the sky
filled with cool, cascading water.

At evening
the cool air rubs my back
I listen to the bees
working for their honey

and the sunset pours light
over my head like a waterfall.

The Space Explorer's Story

Having locked ourselves
airtight in the capsule cockpit,
having checked precisely
that all the instruments said
'GO!'

We flew
beyond the pull of gravity
beyond our own imaginations
deeper into space.

Tons of it swirled around us
filled up to the brim with darkness
and absolutely nothing more.

After several years
of exhaustive exploration
and many detailed surveys
of large meteors and planets
we discovered that we were

spinning round and round in blackness
totally alone.

Mister Moore

Mister Moore, Mister Moore
Creaking down the corridor.

Uh uh eh eh uh
Uh uh eh eh uh

Mister Moore wears wooden suits
Mister Moore's got great big boots
Mister Moore's got hair like a brush
And Mister Moore don't like me much.

Mister Moore, Mister Moore
Creaking down the corridor.

Uh uh eh eh uh
Uh uh eh eh uh

When my teacher's there I haven't got a care
I can do my sums, I can do gerzinters
When Mister Moore comes through the door
Got a wooden head filled with splinters.

Mister Moore, Mister Moore
Creaking down the corridor.

Uh uh eh eh uh
Uh uh eh eh uh

Mister Moore I implore
My earholes ache, my head is sore
Don't come through that classroom door.
Don't come through that classroom door.

Mister Moore, Mister Moore
Creaking down the corridor.

Uh uh eh eh uh
Uh uh eh eh uh

Big voice big hands
Big feet he's a very big man
Take my advice, be good be very very nice
Be good be very very nice
Mister Moore, Mister Moore
Creaking down the corridor.

Uh uh eh eh uh
Uh uh eh eh uh

Mister Moore wears wooden suits
Mister Moore's got great big boots
Mister Moore's got hair like a brush
And Mister Moore don't like me much.

Mister Moore, Mister Moore
Creaking down the corridor.

Uh uh eh eh uh
Uh uh eh eh uh

Winter Morning: Winter Night

This morning I walked to school
through the dark
it was so cold my shadow shivered
under the street lamps.

My feet cracked the ice
that glittered as hard as the frosted stars
stuck on the sky's blue back.

Cars crept by like giant cats
their bright eyes shining.

Tonight I walked over the snow
the moon's cool searchlight
splashed its glow over the garden.

Picking out details of rooftops and hedges
as clearly and sharply
as a summer stillness just after dawn.

Cars on the street roared like lions
bounding over the wet tarmac.

13

Some Days

Some days this school
is a huge concrete sandwich
squeezing me out like jam.

It weighs so much
breathing hurts, my legs freeze
my body is heavy.

On days like that
I carry whole buildings
high on my back.

Other days
the school is a rocket
thrusting right into the sun.

It's yellow and green
freshly painted,
the cabin windows
gleam with laughter.

On days like that
whole buildings support me,
my ladder is pushing
over their rooftops.

Amongst the clouds
I'd need a computer
to count all the bubbles
bursting aloud in my head.

Magic the Rabbit

My rabbit is called Magic
Not just because he wrinkles his nose
And carrots disappear.

Not just because
He wriggles right under the straw
At the back of his hutch
And he disappears.

Not just because
Every time my football team wins
He leaps up and down.

But because last week
He turned the milkman into a frog
The paper girl into a walrus
The postman into a purple jelly
The dustman into a giant lemon
And made my mum and dad
King and Queen of all the World
And me Prime Minister.

'That's magic, Magic,' we cheered
Once we'd wished them all back again.
'Really magic.'

Miss Smith's Garden Secret

Last Saturday we helped Miss Smith and this is what she said:
'Please do some weeding by the path, but don't look in the shed!'

As we dug into the earth, the ground began to quake,
we saw the walls of Miss Smith's shed tremble, wobble, shake.

Clouds of smoke and gusts of fire from underneath the door
scorched our wellies, made them burn until our toes were sore.

'What's in there, Miss?' we all yelled, as we dropped our trowels,
then from deep inside the shed came fearsome grunts and growls.

'It's just my pet,' she tried to smile, 'please don't look inside,'
but with a bang the roof flew off, the door burst open wide.

We didn't know just what we'd see, but thought it would be big,
perhaps a monster or a dragon, but not a guinea pig!

It had a test tube in each paw, it seemed a bit upset,
'That experiment went wrong,' it said, 'but I'll perfect it yet.'

We come top in science now, thanks to our secret teacher,
a real Boff, a real Prof, Miss Smith's amazing creature!

Dobbo's First Swimming Lesson

Dobbo's fists
spiked me to the playground wall
nailed me to the railings.

The plastic ball
he kicked against my skinny legs
on winter playtimes

Bounced a stinging red-hot bruise
across the icy tarmac.

The day we started swimming
we all jumped in
laughed and splashed, sank beneath
the funny tasting water.

Shivering in a corner
Dobbo crouched, stuck to the side,
sobbing like my baby brother
when all the lights go out.

Good Morning!

It's my first morning away from home
my first morning in this hotel
I slept really well, so did Teddy
once we had dropped off to sleep
around three in the morning
because Darren and Brett kept laughing
Ben was snoring
and James was whispering scary ghost stories
but now I'm awake
so I've put on my new jogging bottoms
my new T-shirt, my new jacket
my new gloves, my baseball hat
and my cagoule
I'm ready for anything, even though today
is the fourth of June
and the morning sun is shining over the sea
in flat golden patches
where the gulls bob and swoop
and cry like babies
and everywhere is still and calm and peaceful
mainly because it's half past six in the morning
and breakfast isn't until eight o'clock
there's nothing to do
so I'll sing very loudly, wake everyone up
see if the teachers slept well like me.

Diwali

Winter stalks us
like a leopard in the mountains
scenting prey.

It grows dark,
bare trees stick black bars
across the moon's silver eye.

I will light my lamp for you
Lakshmi,
drive away the darkness.

Welcome you into my home
Lakshmi,
beckon you from every window

With light that blazes
out like flames
across the sombre sky.

Certain houses
crouch in shadow, do not hear
your gentle voice.

Will not feel
your gentle heartbeat
bring prosperity and fortune.

Darkness hunts them
like a leopard in the mountains
stalking prey.

Rudolph's Story

Last night as we practised for Christmas
Old Santa got carried away
Looping the loop over Yorkshire
He fell right out of the sleigh.

We saw him float down through the sky
As the town far below lay asleep
We saw him open his parachute
Then land in a compost heap.

At last we found the right garden
All we saw were his boots in the air
It took him a time but he struggled free
With cabbage leaves stuck in his hair.

'I've lost all my keys!' he shouted.
'From my pocket during my fall
The keys that open the workshop door
We won't have a Christmas at all!'

We started to dig through the compost
The terrible smell made us sneeze
We jumped a mile when a little voice said,
'Please, are you looking for these?'

She stood there holding some keys
They glowed with Santa's power
'I'm Sally,' she said, 'here take them back
Then Santa, please have a shower!'

He clapped his hands and cried, 'Thank you
Now I can fill up my sack
I tell you what, Sally, for a reward
Jump on to Rudolph's back.'

She felt as light as a snowflake
You should've heard us all yell
We zoomed past the stars, halfway to Mars
Happy, in spite of the smell.

On Christmas Eve we found Sally
Fast asleep in her bed
We left her a sack bursting with gifts
And a note from Santa which said:

'Dear Sally, you really saved Christmas
It wasn't some wonderful dream
From all of us here, we'll see you next year
Welcome to Santa's team!'

We Lost Our Teacher to the Sea

We've been at the seaside all day
collecting shells, drawing the view
doing science in the rockpools.

Our teacher went to find the sea's edge,
and stayed there, he's sitting on a rock
he won't come back.

His glasses are frosted over with salt
his beard has knotted into seaweed
his black suit is covered in limpets.

He's staring into the wild water
singing to the waves
sharing a joke with the herring gulls.

We sent out the coastguard
the lifeboat and the orange helicopter
he told them all to go away.

We're getting on the bus with our sticks of rock
our presents for Mum
and our jotters and pencils.

He's still out there as we leave
arms outstretched to the pale blue sky
the tide racing towards him.

His slippery fishtail flaps
with a flick and a shimmer he's gone
back to the sea for ever.

Barry's Budgie . . . Beware!

Dave's got a dog the size of a lion
Half-wolf, half-mad, frothing with venom
It chews up policemen and then spits them out
But it's nothing to the bird I'm talking about.

Claire's got a cat as wild as a cheetah
Scratching and hissing, draws blood by the litre
Jumps high walls and hedges, fights wolves on its own
But there's one tough budgie it leaves well alone.

Murray my eel has teeth like a shark
Don't mess with Murray, he'll zap out a spark
But when Barry's budgie flies over the houses
Murray dims down his lights, blows his own fuses.

This budgie's fierce, a scar down its cheek
Tattoos on its wings, a knife in its beak
Squawks wicked words, does thing scarcely legal
Someone should tell Barry, it's really an eagle.

A Televised Surprise

Imagine our delight
Consternation and surprise
Our teacher on *Come Dancing*
Right before our eyes.

She wore a dress of sequins
That glittered like a flight
Of silent, silver snowflakes
On a winter's night.

She really looked fantastic
No one could ignore
The magic of her dancing
Across the ballroom floor.

Her partner, tall and smart
Only saw him from the back,
Oily hair slicked down short
His suit and shoes were black.

He whirled and twirled her round
As the music got much faster
And then he faced the camera
It was our headmaster!

They seemed to dance for ever
Having so much fun
And then the competition stopped
The pair of them had won.

My Dad's a Stuntman

Some dads work on buses
others work on trains
or pound the beat with great flat feet
or mend and clean the drains.

Some dads dig with shovels
others sail the sea
some are cooks, or publish books
have chat shows on TV.

But my dad
jumps off the top of a giant skyscraper, lands
THUMP on a car roof, rolls over and leaps
through a stack of blazing tyres, dives
on to a motorbike and roars up the road.

Some dads sing in choirs
others play guitars
some have naps, or gaze at maps
or planets, moons and stars.

Some dads play at football
others like to draw
some relax with books of facts
or paint the kitchen door.

But my dad
sleeps curled up on a bed of rusty nails, swims
across an icy pool a hundred times before breakfast,
sets fire to himself and falls out of a plane.
All in a day's work to my dad.

What Marcus the Guard Did One Snowy Night

I'm the Roman
who built a snowman
smack in the centre of Hadrian's wall.

Ghostly and white,
patrolling the night
keeping us safe from Scot, Pict and Gaul.

Icy and strong,
it didn't last long
when my centurion started to rave.

'Marcus, you clown,
now just knock it down
or I'll send you home in chains like a slave!'

Decimated, decapitated
wrecked really rotten, really downgraded
bashed, smashed and thumped
totalled and dumped
lost his ears, eyes and nose
in the deep drift of snows
that was the end
of my frozen friend.

But I don't care
because

I'm the Roman
who built a snowman
smack in the centre of Hadrian's wall

so there!

When Mum Takes Me Football Training

Mum gets out her old bike and pedals like crazy
she makes me run to the park,

I get red-faced and breathless.
When we arrive we play one against one
she picks up the football and kicks it hard
as high as a bird in the big blue sky
it floats up there like a lost balloon,
comes thundering down and I say to myself
'Do I dare head it? Do I? Yes!'
But I don't and I miss it, nearly fall over
and head it back on the fourth bounce
better still trap it, twist past three defenders
and run like a dart for the penalty spot

draw back my foot and belt it for goal.
My mum does her arms-stretched, starfish-shaped

leap-like-a-cat-save, and tips it just round the post
we sit and laugh, then buy an ice cream
take our time going home.

When Dad Took Me Football Training

He put on his new trainers
he put on his new jogging bottoms
he put his fancy new football
in the car with the dog.
We drove to the park three streets away.
I got out and went in goal
I stood there for ages.
Dad kicked the ball
the dog pushed it back

Dad toe-poked the ball
the dog shoved it back
Dad tapped the ball
the dog rolled it back.
The sun came out. The dog rolled over.
Dad lay on the grass and went to sleep.

I flicked the ball on my right foot with my left
kept it off the ground for twenty-five kicks
it dropped from my chest to my knee to my foot
I booted it hard into Dad's back
he grunted
which woke the dog and it barked down his ear
so we all got into the car
and drove home.

Great-Gran Is Manic on Her Motorbike

Shout out loud, say what you like
Great-Gran is manic on her motorbike.

Last week her helmet touched the stars
when she zoomed over thirty cars
she didn't quibble, didn't fuss
when they added a double-decker bus.

Shout out loud, say what you like
Great-Gran is manic on her motorbike.

She's a headline hunting, bike stunting
wacky-wild-one-woman-show
she revs and roars to wild applause
there is no place her bike won't go
she gives them shivers jumping rivers
and balancing across high wires
with a cheer she changes gear
flies her bike through blazing tyres.

Shout out loud, say what you like
Great-Gran is manic on her motorbike.

She told me when she quits bike-riding
she's going to take up paragliding
I'll always be her greatest fan
my dazzling, daredevil, manic Great-Gran!

The Inspectors' Report

Strengths of the school
The tiles in the entrance hall are very shiny
all the footballs in the PE store were full of air
on Tuesday we saw a dinner lady smile.
The white lines on the yard are straight
except when they are supposed to be curvy
the paints in the cupboards are very colourful
and the glue in the glue pots is very sticky.

Weaknesses of the school
Year Three, Year Four, Year Five and Year Six
know very little
English, science or mathematics
also they appear to be
entirely ignorant of music,
geography, history, technology,
PE, RE and ICT
though the little so and so's
achieve very high standards
in tricks with yo-yos.

Year Six
These really are
the worst class we have ever seen!
We mean EVER.
In the entire WORLD.
Their teacher agrees
he's just resigned!

Key points for action
Once we have found where
the head teacher is hiding
we'll let him know.

The Lone Teacher

We've got a new teacher
he wears a mask
and a big wide hat.

He comes to school
on a silver horse
and rides around the field
all day.

Sometimes he says,
'Have you seen Toronto?'

We tell him
we haven't been to Canada
but is it near
the Panama Canal
we did that in geography
last term?

At four o'clock
he rides off into the sunset
and comes back the next morning
in a cloud of dust.

We wonder if
he will ever come and teach us maths
like he said he would
when he first arrived.

Perhaps then he'll tell us his name
not keep it a secret
because my dad always asks me,
'Who is that man?'

Lost in Space

When the spaceship first landed
nose down in Dad's prize vegetables.
I wasn't expecting the pilot
to be a large blue blob with seven heads
the size and shape of rugby balls
and a toothy grin on his fourteen mouths.

'Is this Space Base Six?' he asked.
'No,' I said, 'it's our back garden, number fifty-two.'
'Oh,' he said, 'are you sure?'
and took from his silver overalls
a shiny book of maps.

There were routes round all the galaxies
ways to the stars through deepest space
maps to planets I'd never heard of
maps to comets, maps to moons
and short cuts to the sun.

'Of course,' he said, 'silly me,
I turned right, not left, at Venus,
easily done, goodbye.'
He shook his heads, climbed inside,
the spaceship roared into the sky
and in a shower of leeks and cabbages
disappeared for ever.

Two Traffic Wardens Talking
on Christmas Eve

Nabbed any good ones yet?
Too right I have, a big fat geezer
with a white beard, wearing a red suit
and he's only try to park
some kind of open truck on a double yellow line.

So you says to him push off?
Too right I did, I says to him, 'Oi
what do you think you are playing at here, old son? Eh?
This is a restricted zone, you can't park that thing here
especially with all those animals.'

Animals? What animals?
Horrible great big deer things with vicious horns
and he keeps laughing and saying 'Ho Ho Ho!'
I says to him, 'You'll soon stop laughing
when I write out this parking ticket, old lad.'

Nice one, Stan, so what happened then?
One of those nasty great deer things
really ugly looking he was, with a shiny red hooter
only goes and eats my parking ticket
and tries to eat the rest of the pad as well as my hat.

Cheeky so and so, I hope you told him what for.
I did, I can tell you, I says, 'Oi! What's your game then?'
And he turns round and goes 'Ho Ho Ho!' back at me
tells me he's some kind of van driver
with a load of kids' toys and stuff to deliver.

So what? A double yellow line's a double yellow line.
Exactly, I soon told him, silly old fool
looked him straight in the eye and wrote out a ticket
on the back of a shopping list I had handy.
'Who do you think you are?' I said. 'Father Christmas?'

Alone

The sun has been punctured
sagged out of sight behind the clouds.

I'm alone in the house
watching the moon lay long, cold fingers

On to the curtains and through the glass
in the creaking windows.

If the footsteps outside come up the path
I'm going to hide under my bed.

If the hand I can hear tapping a key
turns the lock and opens the door

I'm going to scamper along the landing
shove the bolt tight on the bathroom door.

If the voice I can hear breathing hard
hisses and whispers up the stairs

I'm going to scramble down the drainpipe
and run for cover in the back garden.

Monsters are clever, those two for example
set their trap by calling my name

In the exact voice of my dad home from work
and of my mum back from the shops.

But I know their tricks, they won't catch me
although I suppose not many monsters

Bang and kick on the bathroom door
yelling, 'Why at eleven years of age

Do we still have to go through this nonsense
each time one of us nips to the shops?'

Perhaps I've got it wrong
again.

My Mum's Put Me on the Transfer List

On Offer:
one nippy striker, ten years old
has scored seven goals this season
has nifty footwork and a big smile
knows how to dive in the penalty box
can get filthy and muddy within two minutes
guaranteed to wreck his kit each week
this is a FREE TRANSFER
but he comes with running expenses
weeks of washing shirts and shorts
socks and vests, a pair of trainers
needs to scoff huge amounts
of chips and burgers, beans and apples
pop and cola, crisps and oranges
endless packets of chewing gum.
This offer open until the end of the season
I'll have him back then
at least until the cricket starts.
Any takers?

Our Tree

It takes so long for a tree to grow
So many years of pushing the sky.

Long branches stretch their arms
Reach out with their wooden fingers.

Years drift by, fall like leaves
From green to yellow then back to green.

Since my grandad was a boy
And then before his father's father

There's been an elm outside our school
Its shadow long across our playground.

Today three men ripped it down.
Chopped it up. It took ten minutes.

Will It Go to a Replay?

Last night's cup-tie
West Ham and Sheffield United
was so exciting, really tough.

Two teams battled it out
through the rain and mud
as goal after goal
thudded into the net.

The crowd went wild
just loved
every nail-biting moment

Four-four
with five minutes left
of extra time
both teams down to nine men
and the tension tightening.

In those dying minutes
both sides
cleared their goal lines
with desperate headers.

West Ham missed a penalty
United missed an open goal.

With seconds to go
a replay at Bramall Lane
seemed certain, until

West Ham had to go in for her tea
and Sheffield United went to the shops
for his mum.

Funny Faces

Just as my teacher's hand
Grips the piece of chalk and he turns
I slip into my act.

If it's just the date he's writing
I do my Gorilla-Eating-A-Rotten-Banana face
Or my Dracula's-Fangs-Sink-Into-Your-Neck face
Or perhaps my Giant-Alien-With-An-Exploding-Head
Which usually gets Kirsty giggling.

If he starts to talk out loud
As he's writing, explaining things carefully
It means I've got a little longer.

Then it's my Monster-Rising-From-The-Stinking-Swamp
And-Reaching-Out-With-Its-Jagged-Claws routine
My Goggle-Eyed-Robot-About-To-Eat-Our-Teacher
And-Spit-Out-The-Bones impression
My Extra-Scary-Ghost-With-The-Silent-Howl
   expression.
Or I do The-Evil-Goblin-Looks-Round-The-Class
Tugging-Hard-At-Its-Ears-Making-Them-Stick-Out act.

Not to mention the Cross-Eyed-Zombie-With-A-Pointed-
   Tongue
Leaping-From-The-Highest-Tower-Of-A-Haunted Castle
Hoping-To-Land-On-The-Unfortunate-Kirsty-Sitting-
   Next-To-Him
But-Just-Missing-And-Vanishing-Over-A-Very-High-Cliff
Landing-Splat-On-The-Cruel-Spiky-Rocks-Below
   routine.

That's a new one I tried this morning
It worked well, got lots of laughs
But sadly our teacher turned round too quickly
And now I'm doing an impersonation
Of me staying in all dinner time
Writing Why I Should Not Pull Silly Faces In Class
Over and over.

At least it gives me plenty of time
To practise some more.

Who Is My Neighbour?

From Jerusalem to Jericho
the road was lonely, narrow, slow.

A man came walking down the track
as thieves crept up behind his back.

They knocked him down and beat his head
stripped him, robbed him, left for dead.

He lay there bleeding in the dirt
moaning, groaning, badly hurt.

The sun burned down, his throat ran dry
but then a priest came passing by.

'Water please,' cried out the man.
'Priest, help me any way you can.'

No help came, he was denied
the priest walked by on the other side.

A second priest ignored his plight
just walked away and out of sight.

As a Samaritan drew near
he shouted out in pain and fear,

'My wife and children will grieve for me
I am in the hands of my enemy.'

But with those hands his wounds were bathed
they raised him up and he was saved.

Carried as a donkey's load
to an inn along the road.

Washed and bandaged, laid to sleep
two silver coins left for his keep.

'Take care of him,' said his new friend,
'I'll pay whatever else you spend

And when he wakes let him know
I was his neighbour not his foe.'

Sir Guy and the Enchanted Princess

Through howling winds on a storm-tossed moor
Sir Guy came to a castle door.

He was led by some strange power
To the deepest dungeon of a ruined tower.

A princess sat on a jewelled throne
Her lovely features carved in stone.

His body trembled, was she dead?
Then her sweet voice filled his head.

'These evil spirits guard me well
Brave Sir Knight, please break their spell.

Though I am stone, you shall see
Kiss me once, I shall be free.'

As demons howled she came to life
Blushed and whispered, 'Have you a wife?'

'My love,' he said, 'still remains
With collecting stamps and spotting trains

But as long as you do as you're told.
I think you'll do, come on, it's cold.'

'Oh,' she cried, 'you weedy bore,
I wish I was entranced once more.'

Lightning struck, the demons hissed
Sir Guy was stone, a voice croaked 'Missed!'

The princess rode his horse away
And poor Sir Guy's still there today.

What the Mountains Do

What the mountains do is
roar silent warnings over
huge brown and heather-covered spaces

or fill up valleys with dark green laughter

before resting their stone-cropped heads
in sunlight.

Lion

Great rag bag
jumble-headed thing
shakes its mane
in a yawn that turns to anger,
teeth picked out like stalactites
in some vast cave
bone-grinders, flesh-rippers
hyena bringers, jackal callers
and huge paws
the size of death
clamp down on antelope,
later, sleeping through the night
each star a lion
flung with pride across a sky
black as a roaring mouth
lion dreams of open spaces
dreams the smell of freedom.

· Lion ·

All of Us Knocking on the Stable Door

Three great kings, three wise men
Tramp across the desert to Bethlehem
Arrive at the inn, don't travel no more
They start knocking at the stable door.

Knocking at the door, knocking at the door
All of us are knocking at the stable door.

I've got myrrh, he's got gold
He's got frankincense and all of us are cold
We stand here shivering, chilled to the core
We're just knocking on the stable door.

The star above it glows in the sky
Burning up the darkness and we know why
A baby king's asleep in the straw
So we start knocking on the stable door.

Travelled some distance, we've travelled far
Melchior, Casper and Balthazaar
We are so wealthy, the baby's so poor
But here we are knocking on the stable door.

Now is the time, now is the hour
To feel the glory, worship the power
We quietly enter, kneel on the floor
Just the other side of the stable door.

Knocking on the door, knocking on the door
All of us knocking at the stable door.

Knocking on the door, knocking on the door
We're all knocking at the stable door.

Nights Out with Gaz

A night out with Gaz
was over the wall
and into a castle
bigger than Camelot.

The tower burned
silver with moonlight,
we'd sit in the arch
of a window talking.

Then back to his house
for mystery tins
bought cheap with no labels
by his mum from the market.

Two mugs of tea
and beans on toast
or maybe rice pudding
prunes or dog meat.

Next morning with Mick
we'd deliver the papers,
the man in the shop
thought we were daft.

'You ought to grow up
not make stupid noises
in the castle at midnight,
lads of your age.'

I'd think of that tower
pale as a ghost ship
silence hanging
like mist round the mast.

Why grow up
and have to leave Camelot;
why always know
that this time it's beans?

There's Very Little Merit in a Ferret

There's very little merit in a ferret
Whipping up your trouser leg
Very little merit in a ferret
Whipping up your trouser leg

If it were a pine marten
Oh boy you'd be smarting
If it were a puma, you'd be dead

There's very little merit in a ferret
Whipping up your trouser leg

So if you dote on a stoat
If your heart goes blink for a mink
If you play footloose
With a mongoose
If you potter with an otter
If you beazel with a weasel
If your heart is set
On a marmoset
Then think

There's very little merit in a ferret
Whipping up your trouser leg

Ferret, stoats they are vermin
You don't want your underpants
Trimmed with ermine

There's very little merit in a ferret
Whipping up your trouser leg.

*P.S. When I wrote this poem I made a mistake. I
thought a marmoset was a type of ferret-like creature. It
isn't. It's a small monkey. I meant a marmot . . . which
of course is a small type of Bovril.*

Dazzling Derek

That's my dad shouting at me
from the touchline
like he does every game we play.

I don't know why
I think we do quite well really
this week we're only losing ten-one
and I've scored three times
twice in my goal
and once in theirs

not bad for a goalie.

Last week I was on the wing
it was brilliant
I nearly scored a million times
we still lost
but who was counting?

My dad was
he got really angry
there's no pleasing him.

What he really wants to do
is to shrink back to being ten like me
slip onto the field
score the winning goal
with seconds to go
defeat staring us in the face
Dazzling Derek saves the day!

But he can't
so he jumps up and down on the touchline
shouts at me
mutters and kicks the grass
stubs his toe and yells
nearly gets sent off the field by the ref

where's the fun in that?

Living with Cats

The cat's shadow
stretches a thin dark rope
along the white wall.

And the shrew
snuffles the scent
through its long thin nose.

Knows what it senses.

Goes jittering
        skittering

a ping-pong ball
that wildly bounces

with not enough legs
to escape.

*

The balloon
like a fat pink pawprint
stuck on the sky.

The cats
stretch and yawn
in the tall grass.

Today they
do not care much about balloons
or hot air.
They are whispering
quiet secrets to the mice

who twitch in their tunnels
just out of sight.

*

Next door's spaniel
going ballistic

completely barking.

Cats in the sun
lazy as lions on the garage roof
wave their tails.

Next door's spaniel
must be a springer

up and down
on his pogo-stick legs

howling and snarling
like a pack of bloodhounds.

Cats in the shade
half asleep on next door's patio
stick out their tongues.

*

Maisie and Piglet
have tracked down the doormat
stalked the slidy-slippery rug
and pounced on the carpet.

Those jobs are done
no more trouble there.

Now they are watching the tropical fish tank
like some giant television
they are waiting for the channel to change
to their favourite programme

scuba-diving for kittens.

*

Quickly and quietly
the cat crosses
the great green river
of the settee.

Paw to paw
avoiding the water
by delicate leaps

on the stepping stones
of our sleeping heads.

I'm a Shepherd in the Christmas Play

I've got a long stripy robe
and a scarf on my head
tied with string.

I do a shepherd dance
and give baby Jesus
Darren's toy lamb.

My dad says
he was a shepherd
in his school play once.

He had a dressing gown on
and a tea towel on his head
held on with a snakebelt.

He told me
I couldn't be a proper shepherd
without a dressing gown on.

I told him he was daft
shepherds don't sleep in a bedroom
they have a field.

Anyway, when he did his play
it was so long ago
I bet he saw baby Jesus for himself.

My dad didn't laugh much
when I said that, but my mum
laughed so much she cried.

Busy Brothers, Talented Twins

My twin brother Adam
has just got a job in the circus.

Not on the trapeze or tightrope
he doesn't like heights.

Not as a spangled bareback rider
horses make him sneeze.

Not as a fire-eating juggler
Dad says he mustn't play with matches.

He's become the star attraction
*Adam the Mighty Atom, the World's Youngest
Strongman!*

Last week he balanced Mum on his head
lifted Grandad up in his armchair.

Suspended Dad from his teeth by the braces
Gran swung by her bloomers from his big toe.

They were quite impressed.
'Coo,' they said, 'this is unusual for a six-year-old.'

We saw him in the ring last night
in a plastic leopard-skin vest and his PE shorts.

He twirled an elephant on one finger
pushed a car full of clowns away from his foot.

Ripped up a telephone directory
bent six iron bars and never once dropped his teddy.

He asked me to see tomorrow's show.
'I'm sorry,' I said, 'I'm leaving for Mars at teatime.'

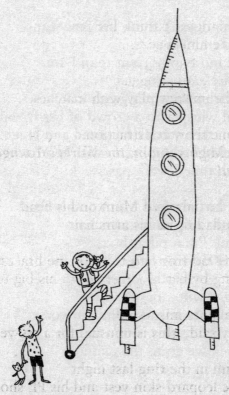

'Life's very busy,' I explained,
'when you're the World's Youngest Astronaut.'

I Want to Be Friends with a Girl Who . . .

Hasn't got slimy lipstick stuck
all over her face
like raspberry jam.

Who doesn't think her new jeans
and trainers
are more important than I am.

A girl who won't giggle
and whisper to a crowd of her friends
then throw back her head and laugh
like a howling hyena with toothache
each time I walk past.

So that my face burns and boils
bright red and passers-by
think I'm a pillar box,
start shoving letters in my mouth.

A girl who doesn't
bring her friend along, or worse
her little sister,
when we go to the pictures.

A girl who doesn't want me to be
eighteen with money
and a hip-hop-top-big-pop-star-hairstyle
dripping with gel.

Hard luck, Jane,
Jan, Fran and Anne.

You aren't Lisa, the girl of my dreams
you're not the ones
who'll get my kisses.

I Want to Be Friends with a Boy Who . . .

Hasn't got a face
full of spots
and a kiss full
of chewing-gum, pickled-onion crisps
and slobber.

A boy who doesn't think
I'm his mother
his nurse
his life-long football fan
or his punchbag.

A boy who hasn't got a head full
of swearing and fighting
of video games that rip bits off you.

And who doesn't smell
of his dad's-I-didn't-really-want-this-
Christmas-present-from-Gran-
aftershave.

Who doesn't forever pick
his nose or pinch
my headband or push
me in the bushes for a laugh.

A boy who isn't riddled
with macho
like holes on a cheese.

Hard luck, Dean,
Shane, Dane and Duane.

You aren't Ryan, the boy of my dreams
you're not the ones
who'll get my kisses.

The Elephant Dictionary

Elegant:
What elephants always are
Especially at dinner.

Elevator:
How elephants go upstairs.

Elocution:
Polite trumpeting.

Elicopter:
Used by the elephant Flying Squad.

Elevision:
Home entertainment for the elephant
(also known as ellytelly).

Elescope:
A long-sighted elephant.

Elepathic:
a far-sighted elephant.

Elephone:
For trunk calls.

Elementary:
Infants school for tiny tuskers.

Elegy:
Sad elephant's song.

Elements:
Rough weather for crossing the Alps.

Eletosis:
Bad breath on an elephant's tongue.

Elligator:
A snappy dresser amongst the pachyderms.

Alien Exchange

We've got an alien at our school
he's on an exchange trip
I'd quite fancy him
if he wasn't so weird looking.
Just one head
only two legs
and no feelers at all
he hasn't got claws on the end of his hands
and he's only got – don't laugh – two eyes.

Can you believe that?
When we first saw him we fell about
but as our teacher says
we must be thoughtful and respect all visitors
to our galaxy
even if they have got only one feeding system
a breathing tube that is much too small
and horrid furry stuff on their head.

Next month my sister and I
are visiting his planet on the exchange.
It's got a funny name, Earth.
We've got to stay two weeks
our teacher says we must be careful
not to tread on the Earthlings by mistake
and always, always be polite
to raise our wings in greeting
and to put rubber tips on our sharpest horns.
I'm not looking forward to it much
the food looks awful
and the sea's dirty, not to mention the air.
Still, it'll make a change from boring old school
and perhaps some alien
will quite fancy me!

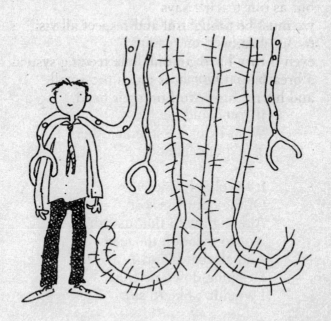

It's Behind You

I don't want to scare you
But just behind you
Is a . . .

No! Don't look!
Just act calmly
As if it wasn't there.

Like I said
Can you hear me if I whisper?
Just behind you
Is a . . .

NO! DON'T LOOK!
Just keep on reading
Don't turn round, believe me
It isn't worth it.

If you could see
What I can see standing there
You'd understand.

It's probably one
Of the harmless sort
Although with that mouth
Not to mention the teeth
And all that blood
Dripping down its chin
I wouldn't like to say.

DON'T TURN ROUND!
Listen
It's trying to speak
I think it wants to be friends.

Oh, I see, it doesn't, never mind
You'd better leave just in case
I expect you'll escape
If you don't look round.

Oh, what a shame!
I thought you'd make it
To the door. Hard luck.
I still think it means no harm.
I expect it eats all its friends.

There's a Monster in the Garden

If the water in your fish pond fizzes and foams
And there's giant teeth marks on the plastic gnomes
You've found huge claw prints in the flower bed
And just caught sight of a two-horned head
Put a stick in your front lawn with a piece of card on
Look out everybody – there's a monster in the garden!

You haven't seen the dustman for several weeks
Haven't seen the gasman who was looking for leaks
Haven't seen the paper-girl, postman or plumber
Haven't seen the window cleaner since last summer
Don't mean to be nosy, I do beg your pardon
Look out everybody – there's a monster in the garden!

One dark night it will move in downstairs
Start living in the kitchen, take you unawares
Frighten you, bite on you, with howls and roars
It will crash about, smash about, push you out of doors
In the cold and snow the ice and rain will harden
Look out everybody – there's a monster in the garden!

Now listen to me, neighbour, all of this is true
It happened next door, now it's happening to you.
There's something nasty on the compost heap
Spends all day there curled up asleep
You don't want your bones crunched or jarred on
Look out everybody – there's a monster in the garden!

Pasting Patsy's Pasty Posters

Petra Porter pastes in precincts
Patsy's pasty pasties posters
Patsy's posters from her pasties
and her tasty pasty pasta.

Patsy pays a pretty penny
for Petra's posters in the precincts
but Paula pastes her posters faster
passes Petra, pasting past her.

So Patsy's pasting Paula's posters
paying pasty Paula plenty
for faster pasta poster pasting
pasting pasta posters faster.

Flight from Planet Earth

Landing here because we had to
the fuel gone and the computers broken
we crashed into a bank of sand
let the dust die down
then climbed out of our rocket.

We were surrounded by eyes
along the rim of the distant mountains
in the desert at our feet,
it was worse at night
when they glowed like fires
staring at us without blinking.

Time has passed
we live in the wreck of our spacecraft
eat what is left of our stores
drink rainwater
sometimes we go out looking for food,
the creatures always force us back
make us afraid,
we are the aliens here
and they don't like us.

The Visitor

It was late last night I'm certain
wasn't it?
That I saw my bedroom curtain
twitch and flutter
felt a chill, heard him mutter,
'Hello, lad, I'm back.'

Uncle Jack
dead since this night last year
wasn't it?
A pickled onion in his beer
stopped his breath, a sudden death
that took us sadly by surprise.

But there he was, those eyes
one grey, one blue
one through
which the light could pass
the other, glass.

He drifted down, swam about
didn't he?
In his brown suit, flat cap, stout
boots and tie
I saw him remove his eye
didn't I?

'It's not a dream
this,' he said, 'don't scream
I'll not come back, I shan't return,'
then I felt the ice-cold burn
of his glass eye on my skin.
Saw his ghastly ghostly grin,
'Don't worry, don't get in a stew,
just thought I'd keep an eye on you.'

When I woke up today
I saw the blue eye not the grey.
But when I picked it up to go
it drained away like melting snow.
Didn't it?

Harry Hobgoblin's Superstore

You want a gryphon's feather
Or a spell to change the weather?
A pixilating potion
To help you fly an ocean?
Some special brew of magic
To supercharge your broomstick?
Witches, wizards, why not pop
Into Harry's one-stop shop?

Tins of powdered dragon's teeth,
Bottled beetles, newts.
Freeze-dried cobwebs, cats and rats,
Screaming mandrake roots.
Lizard skins, stirred widdershins,
A giant's big toenail,
Second-hand spells used only once
New ones that can't fail.
Spells to grow some donkey's ears
On the teacher no one likes,
Spells to make you good at sums,
Spells to find lost bikes.

Spells that grow and stretch and shrink,
Spells that make your best friend stink,
Sacks of spells stacked on my shelves,
Come on in, see for yourselves.
Magical prices, tricks galore
At Harry Hobgoblin's Superstore.

Slick Nick's Dog's Tricks

Slick Nick's dog does tricks
the tricks Nick's dog does are slick
he picks up sticks, stands on bricks
Nick's finger clicks, the dog barks *SIX!*
He picks a mix of doggy bix
then gives Slick Nick thick sloppy licks.
Mick and Rick's dog's not so quick
kicks the bricks, drops the sticks
can't bark to six, is in a fix
gets Mick and Rick to do its tricks
gets on their wicks despite its mix
of waggy tail and loving licks
but Slick Nick's dog does tricks
the tricks Nick's dog does are slick.

Index of First Lines

A night out with Gaz   57
Dave's got a dog the size of a lion   24
Dobbo's fists   17
Elegant   74
From Jerusalem to Jericho   49
Great rag bag   54
Hasn't got a face   72
Hasn't got slimy lipstick stuck   70
Having locked ourselves   9
He put on his new trainers   31
I don't want to scare you   78
If the water in your fish pond fizzes and foams   80
I'm the Roman   27
Imagine our delight   25
It takes so long for a tree to grow   44
It was late last night I'm certain   84
It's my first morning away from home   18
I've got a long stripy robe   66
Just as my teacher's hand   47
Landing here because we had to   83
Last night as we practised for Christmas   21
Last night's cup-tie   45
Last Saturday we helped Miss Smith and this is
    what she said   16
Mister Moore, Mister Moore   10
Mum gets out her old bike and pedals like crazy   29
My rabbit is called Magic   15
My twin brother Adam   68
Nabbed any good ones yet?   39
On a blue day   8
On Offer   43

Petra Porter pastes in precincts   82
Shout out loud, say what you like   33
Slick Nick's dog does tricks   88
Some dads work on buses   26
Some days this school   14
Strengths of the school   34
That's my dad shouting at me   61
The cat's shadow   63
The sun has been punctured   41
The twelfth of December 1231   7
There's very little merit in a ferret   59
This morning I abolished   5
This morning I walked to school   12
Three great kings, three wise men   55
Through howling winds on a storm-tossed moor   51
What the mountains do is   53
We've been at the seaside all day   23
We've got a new teacher   36
We've got an alien at our school   76
When the spaceship first landed   38
Winter stalks us   19
You want a gryphon's feather   86